HOLT SOCIAL STUDIES
PEOPLE

JoAnn Cangemi
General Editor

HOLT, RINEHART AND WINSTON, PUBLISHERS
New York • Toronto • Mexico City • London • Sydney • Tokyo

General Editor
JoAnn Cangemi

is Professor of Education and Director of Graduate Studies in Education at Nicholls State University, Thibodaux, Louisiana. She received her Ph.D. in elementary education from Louisiana State University. Prior to her university work, Dr. Cangemi taught in the public elementary schools for ten years. She has served as a consultant in social studies curriculum development to numerous public and private school systems. She is the author of a number of articles in professional journals. For ten summers she taught in Europe as part of a foreign exchange program. She was a 1981 recipient of the Merit Teacher Awards given by the National Council for Geographic Education.

Contributing Writers
James A. Harris

is an elementary principal in the D.C. Everest Area School District, Schofield, Wisconsin. He graduated from Miami University, Oxford, Ohio, and received his Master's degree in Curriculum and Instruction from the University of Wisconsin. Mr. Harris began his teaching career while a VISTA volunteer and later served in the Wisconsin Native American Teacher Corps. For ten years he taught kindergarten and primary grades in Wisconsin schools. Mr. Harris is a frequent consultant to school systems and educational corporations. He has published many articles in professional magazines and journals.

Pat Cuthbertson

is a writer who lives in Santa Cruz, California. She received a B.A. in English literature from the University of California at Santa Cruz, graduating with General College Honors. She has written material for Language Arts and Social Studies texts. She has two sons in whose classes she has worked as a volunteer for several years.

Tom Cuthbertson

is a writer of "how to" books who lives in Santa Cruz, California. He received a B.A. in literature from the University of California at Santa Cruz and an M.A. in writing from San Francisco State. He has written a number of technical manuals, as well as material for Language Arts and Social Studies texts. He has done volunteer work in his sons' elementary school classrooms.

James J. Rawls

is a native of Washington, D.C. He received a B.A. from Stanford University and a Ph.D. from the University of California, Berkeley. Since 1975, Rawls has been a history instructor at Diablo Valley College. His articles and reviews have appeared in such publications as *The Journal of American History, The Wilson Quarterly, The American West,* and *California History.* He is the author of *Indians of California: The Changing Image* and coauthor of *California: An Interpretive History* and *Land of Liberty.* Rawls has served as an historical consultant on numerous films and on a series of television programs funded by the National Endowment for the Humanities.

"The Yellow House," © Janet Munro 1984/Jay Johnson Gallery

Photo and art credits are on page 160.

ISBN:0-03-001778-5
56789 039 9876543

Teacher Consultants

Linda R. Aucoin
Teacher
Thibodaux Elementary School
Thibodaux, Louisiana

Sister Eileen Frances M. Cooke
Teacher
Saint Helena School
Philadelphia, Pennsylvania

Patricia F. Ho
Teacher
Thomas J. Watson, Sr. Elementary
   School
Endicott, New York

Janet A. Kaiser
Teacher
Hawthorne School—District U205
Elmhurst, Illinois

Thomas J. Ladouceur
Teacher
Stone Valley Intermediate School
Alamo, California

Dr. JoAnn B. Seghini
Director of Curriculum Development
Jordan School District
Sandy, Utah

Ramona H. Simpson, M.A.
Teacher
Saffell Elementary
Lawrenceburg, Kentucky

James Robert Warren
Teacher
Tileston School
Wilmington, North Carolina

Content Consultants

Joseph D. Baca
Social Studies Education Specialist
New Mexico Department of Education
Santa Fe, New Mexico

Sam F. Dennard, Ph.D.
Social Studies Coordinator
Clayton County Schools
Jonesboro, Georgia

Dr. George Gregory
Curriculum Consultant
Albany, New York

David M. Helgren, Ph.D.
Assistant Professor
University of Miami
Coral Gables, Florida

Betty Jo Johnson
Coordinator, Social Studies Services
Wake County Public School System
Raleigh, North Carolina

Dr. Helen E. Jones
Associate Professor of Education
Fairmont State College
Fairmont, West Virginia

Diane Lindstrom
Associate Professor of History
University of Wisconsin
Madison, Wisconsin

Eveleen Lorton
Professor of Education
University of Miami
Coral Gables, Florida

Norman McRae
Director of Social Studies Department
Detroit Public Schools
Detroit, Michigan

Thomas H. Pagenhart
Associate Professor of Geography
California State University
Hayward, California

Clyde P. Patton
Professor of Geography
University of Oregon
Eugene, Oregon

Daniel H. Ryan
Professor
College of Lake County
Grayslake, Illinois

Mary Jo Wagner
Director, Women's Studies Program
University of Oregon
Eugene, Oregon

Philip Weeks
Department of History
The University of Akron
Akron, Ohio

Susan A. White
Senior Economics Consultant
Adult Performance Level Project:
   The University of Texas at Austin
Austin, Texas

Readability Consultant

Paul Greenfield
Associate Professor
English and Humanities
Dutchess Community College
Poughkeepsie, New York

TABLE OF CONTENTS

UNIT 1

You and Your Family

You are **special.**
No one else is just like you.
Your **family** is special too.
No other family is like yours.

 # You are Special

Your friends see you.
They hear your voice.
They know it is you.

You like some things.
You do not like other things.
You do things your own way.
That is why you are special.

2 You Have a Name

You have a **name**.
It may be long.
It may be short.

We all have names.
Names help make you special.
You can find names **everywhere**.

15

3 Families Are Special

Look at these families.
They are special too.
Every family is special.

16

 # Your Family Lives in a Special Place

You live at **home.**
Your home is special.
Your home is special to you.
A family makes home a special
place.

This is Rico's room.
Rico likes his room.
He likes all the things in it.

This is a picture of Rico's room.
Can you find Rico's bed?
Can you find the door?

 Families Change

Families **change**.
Families may get bigger.
They may get smaller.

A family may stay the same
size.
But the people may change.

6 People Grow and Change

People **grow** in many ways.
People change in many ways.
People never stay the same.

Look at the red line.
It shows how tall Roy was at three.
Now Roy is six.
Which line shows how tall he
is now?

6 years old

5 years old

4 years old

3 years old

Age

7 Families Learn

You **learn** new things.
Your family helps you learn.
Your family learns from you too.

8 Families Have Rules

A **rule** tells you the right thing to do.
Some rules keep you **safe.**
Some rules help keep a home clean.
Some rules give everyone a turn.

9 Families Share a Language

Families talk **together**.
Some may use special **words**.
What words does your family use for these things?

Some families speak different **languages**.

Others may speak with their
hands.

FAMOUS AMERICANS

The De Bolt Family

The De Bolt family is very big. It has more than 15 children. Most of the children were not born into this family. Henry was born in Africa. Kim and Marty come from Korea. Brenda is a Sioux Indian.

Some of the children cannot walk well. Some cannot see. All the children learn to help one another.

There are a lot of children in the De Bolt family. But there is enough love to go around.

1. Which picture is best for each sentence?

Your family helps you learn.

A family needs a place to live.

Everyone has a name.

We grow and change.

2. Tell a family rule.

UNIT 2

Families: Living and Working Together

Families help each other.
They **work** together.
They play together.
Families **share** many things.

1 Families Have Needs

All people **need** some things.
They need **food**.
They need **clothing**.

People need a home.
They need **love**, too.

You need the right foods to grow.
This picture shows some foods
you need.

THE FOODS

FRUITS	VEGETABLES

The foods are in groups.
You should not eat foods from just
one group.
You should eat foods from each of the groups.

YOU NEED

MEAT OR FISH	BREAD OR CEREAL	MILK FOODS

41

2 Families Meet Their Needs

Families meet their needs
in different ways.
We all need food.
We do not all eat the same food.
We all need a home.
We do not all have the same
kind of house.

We do not all dress the same.
But we all have the same needs.

3 Families Have Wants

Families need things.
They also **want** things.
Sometimes a family must **choose**.

4 Family Members Work

A **job** you do is called work.
People work at many kinds of
jobs.
They may work at home to make
things.

People may work away from home.
People work to **earn** money.
Then they **buy** things they need
or want.

5 You Can Help

Family members help each other.
All of us are good at different things.
But everyone is good at
something.

Your **parents** help you.
You can help your parents.
What jobs can you do well?

49

 # Others Help

Sometimes your family cannot
be with you.
They may be at work.
They may be away.
Other people may help you
then.

Kate is in the hospital.
Her family cannot stay.
Many **workers** are there.
They will take care of Kate.

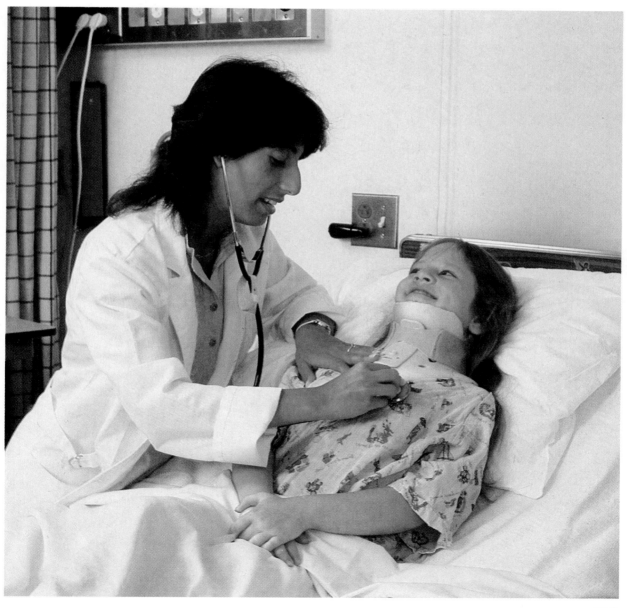

7 Families Spend Time Together

Families have fun together.
This family is at the zoo.
They like to look
at the **animals**.

Find the picture of the lion.
Find the picture of the bear.
What animal is in the water?
What animal is in a tree?

8 Families Celebrate Special Days

A **birthday** is special.
So is a **wedding** day.
They are family times.
Families **celebrate** these days.

This family is together.
They came from many places.
This is their **reunion**.
Everyone likes the visit.
They will be back next year!

FAMOUS AMERICANS
The Wright Brothers

For many years people wanted to fly. They tried many ways. Some people even put feathers on their arms.

Then Wilbur and Orville Wright built a flying machine. At first it did not work. The brothers kept trying. Finally the machine flew.

The brothers told their father. Their father told the newspapers. Their family was proud.

UNIT REVIEW

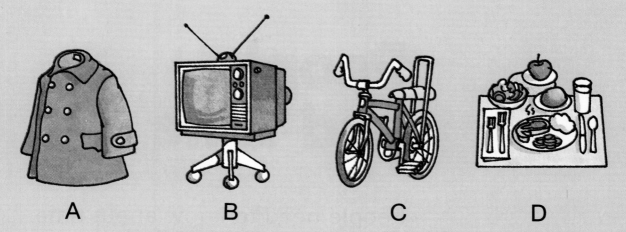

A   B   C   D

1. Look at the pictures above.
   Which are needs?
   Which are wants?
2. Tell how you can help your family.
3. Look at the pictures below.
   Where do the people work?

A

B

UNIT 3

People and Time

People need to know about time.
Look at the pictures.
What things do people use to
tell time?

1 Yesterday, Today, and Tomorrow

This is **yesterday.**
Yesterday is gone.

This is **today.**
Today is now.

This is **tomorrow.**
Tomorrow has not happened yet.

Day and Night

The **earth** looks like a big ball.
The earth turns.
The **sun** shines on the earth.

Only one side of the earth faces
the sun at a time.
That side is **light.**
The other side is **dark.**

The light time is called **day**.

The dark time is called **night.**

Telling Time

A **clock** tells us the time.
The short hand tells the **hours.**
The long hand tells the **minutes.**

Look at the pictures.
What is Tony doing at 8:00 in the
morning?
What is he doing at 11:00?
What is he doing at 4:00?
When does he go to bed?

The Days of the Week

A **week** has seven days.
The days are always in the same order.
Each day has a different name.
Name the days of the week.
What day comes after Saturday?

1 SUNDAY

2 MONDAY

3 TUESDAY

This is Anna.
Anna visits her grandmother on Sunday.
She goes to school on Monday.
Name the four other days Anna goes to school.
What does Anna do on Saturday?

4 WEDNESDAY

5 THURSDAY

6 FRIDAY

7 SATURDAY

69

5 The Months and Seasons

A **year** has 12 **months.**
The first month is January.
Say the names of the months in order.
Which month comes after December?

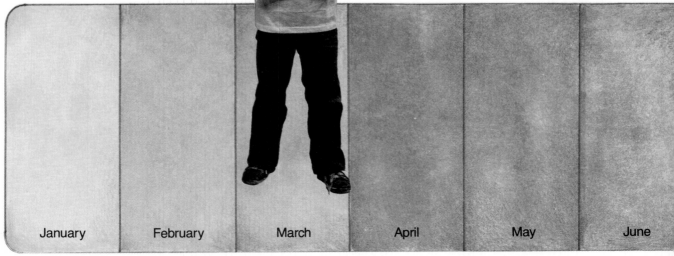

| January | February | March | April | May | June |

Look at the picture.

It shows the months in order.

These children are standing where their birthdays are.

Don's birthday is in March.

When is Terry's birthday?

| July | August | September | October | November | December |

Each year has four **seasons**.
One is **spring**.
One is **summer**.
One is **fall**.
One is **winter**.

DECEMBER

NOVEMBER

OCTOBER

SEPTEMBER

AUGUST

JULY

Find the picture that shows summer.
Find the picture that shows winter.
How is the winter picture different
from the summer picture?

JANUARY

FEBRUARY

MARCH

APRIL

MAY

JUNE

6 Holidays

Holidays are special days.
Holidays come once a year.
Look at the pictures.
What holiday does each one show?
What other holidays can you name?

7 Our Country's Special Days

Martin Luther King wanted people to be free.
He wanted **laws** to be fair to all people.
His birthday is in January.

January						2
3	4	5				9
10	11	12	13	14	15	16
17	18	19	20	21	22	23
24 31	25	26	27	28	29	30

George Washington was a
President.
Abraham Lincoln was one too.
Their birthdays are in February.

We have special days for people.
We also have special days for
special things.
Arbor Day is our tree day.
Some people plant trees.
They show that they love
trees.

This is the **American flag**.
We have a holiday for our
flag.
It is called **Flag Day**.
We celebrate Flag Day on June 14.

RACHEL CARSON

Rachel Carson was a **scientist**. She studied **nature**. She loved nature all her life. She loved how the seasons changed. Rachel Carson worked for the United States. She helped care for rivers and seas.

Rachel Carson wrote about nature. One of her books told how people were hurting the air, land, and sea.

Rachel Carson worked to make a cleaner world.

UNIT REVIEW

1. Name the days of the week.
2. Name the months of the year.
3. Look at the pictures.
   What is the best time to do
   what each child is doing?

12:00   6:00   8:00

Going to School

Eating Dinner   Eating Lunch

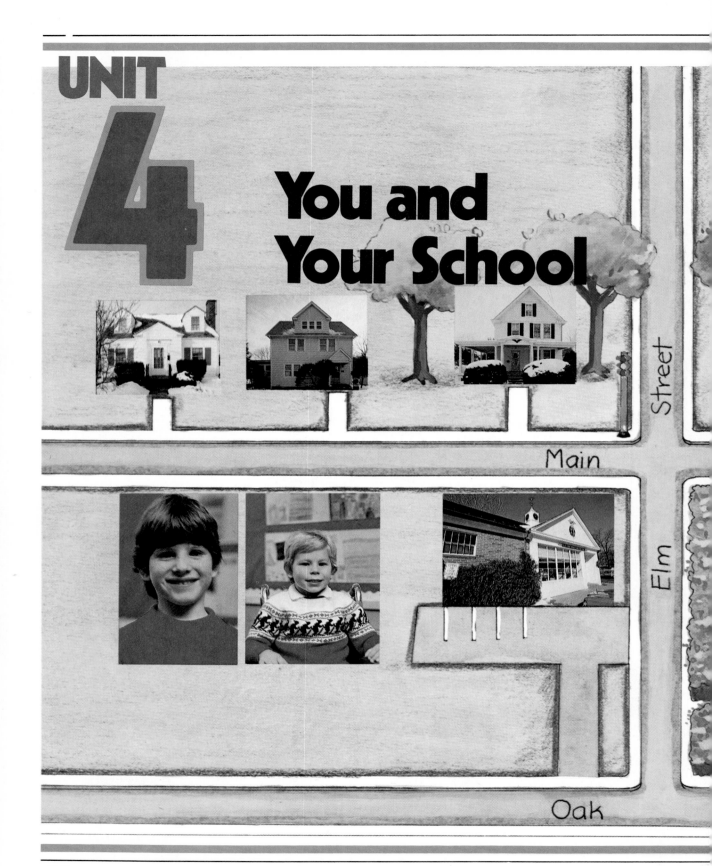

UNIT 4

You and Your School

Street

Main

Elm

Oak

82

Wendy and Scott go to school.
They see many things on the way.
They like to learn new things.
They like to see their friends.

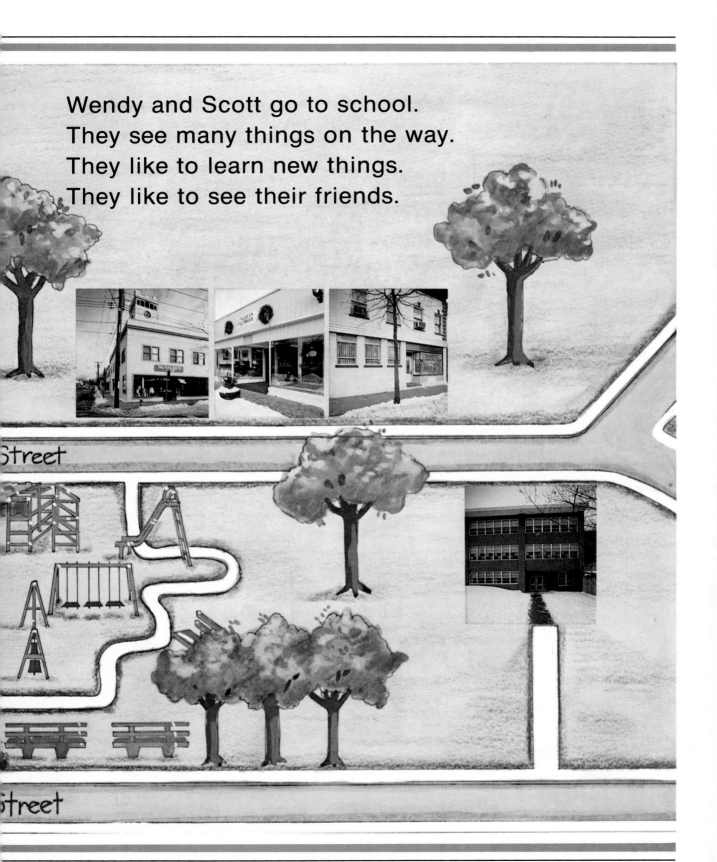

Street

Street

1 Open School Day

Today is Open School Day.
Wendy asks her grandfather
to come.
Wendy gives Grandfather
something to read.
It will help him find the school.

84

Wendy lives **near** the school.
She walks to school every day.
She walks down this **street.**

2 Places on a Map

This is what Wendy gave
Grandfather.
It is a **map.**
A map is a picture of a place.

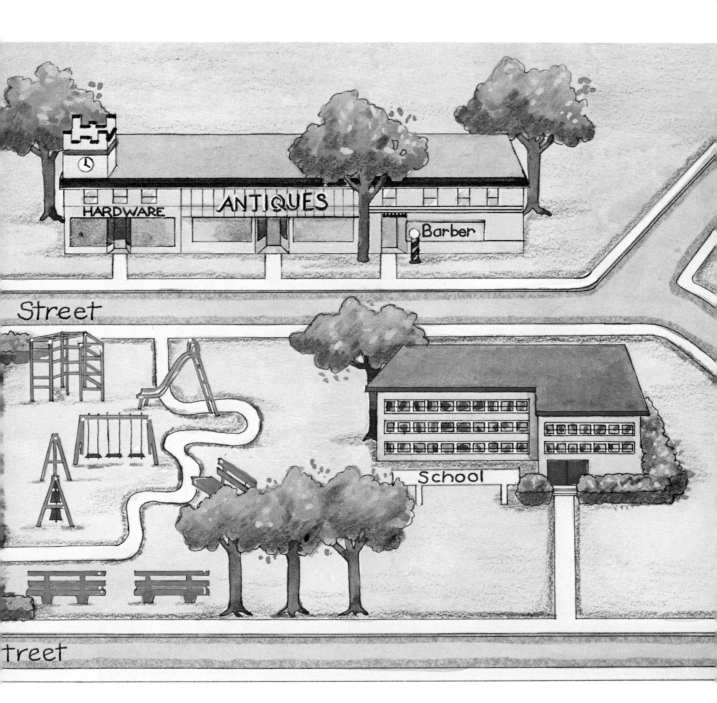

Look at the map.
Find the post office.
Find Wendy's school.
Find the park.

 # Reading a Map

This is a picture of Wendy's house.

This is another kind of picture.
It shows Wendy's house too.

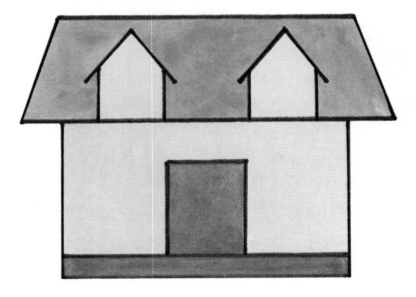

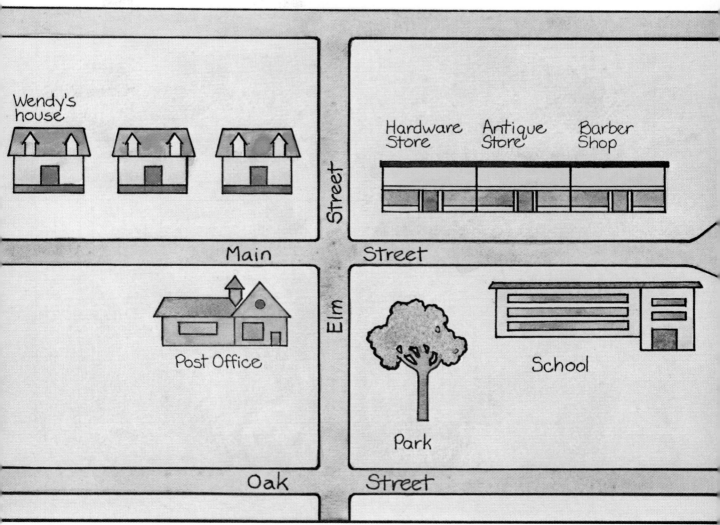

Here is another map.
It shows the same place in a
new way.
This map has pictures too.
The pictures show real places.
Find the picture of Wendy's
house on the map.

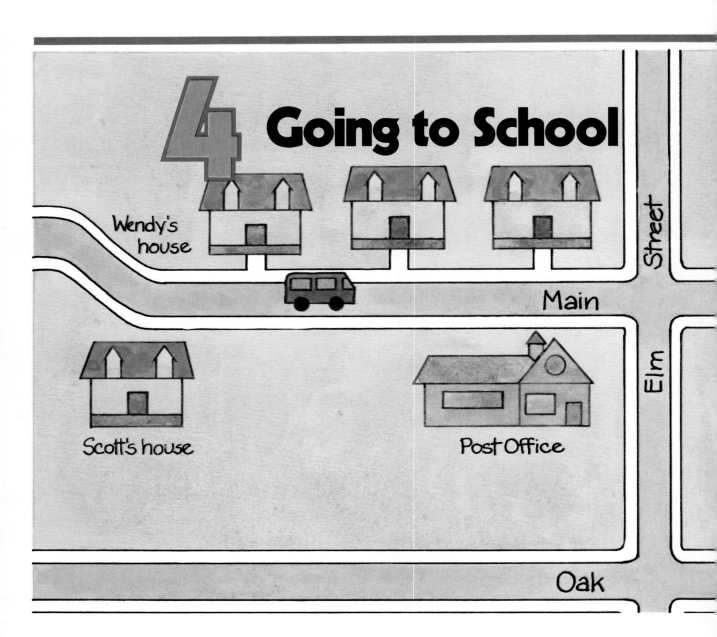

4 Going to School

Wendy's house

Scott's house

Post Office

Street

Main

Elm

Oak

This is Scott.
Scott and Wendy go to the
same school.
Scott rides to school in this bus.

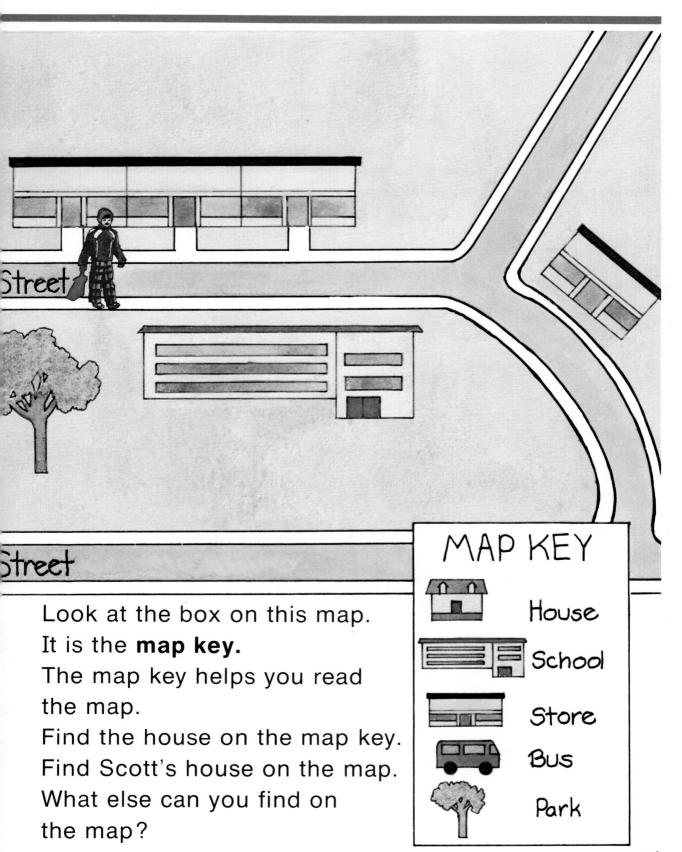

Street

Street

Look at the box on this map.
It is the **map key.**
The map key helps you read
the map.
Find the house on the map key.
Find Scott's house on the map.
What else can you find on
the map?

MAP KEY

House

School

Store

Bus

Park

91

 # At School

Now Wendy and Scott are at school.
Wendy's grandfather is there too.
Many families and friends have come.
They will find out about the school.

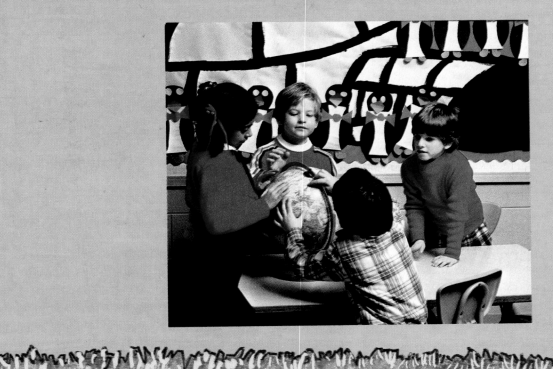

The teacher made a **plan**.
The children will read.
They will do math.
Grandfather says, "It looks
like a busy day."

OUR PLAN

	9:00 A.M.	Reading
	10:00 A.M.	Recess
	10:15 A.M.	Snack
$\frac{\begin{array}{r}6\\+2\end{array}}{8}$ 1+3=4	10:30 A.M.	Math
	11:00 A.M.	Art
	12:00 A.M.	Lunch
	1:00 P.M.	Social Studies
	1:30 P.M.	Science
	2:00 P.M.	Recess
	2:15 P.M.	Writing
	3:00 P.M.	Home

 Schools Have Tools and Machines

The school has many **tools**.
It also has **machines**.
Teachers use tools and
machines to **teach**.

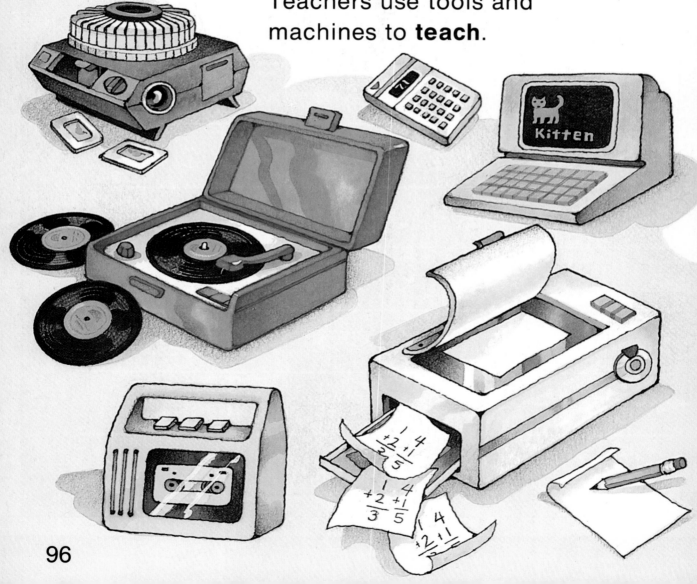

You may use them, too.
Some machines help you learn.

7 Schools Have Rules

Scott tells about rules.
He says, "Our school has rules.
We are quiet in the halls.
We put our things away."

But rules are not just for children.
Rules help all of us.

8 Schools Have Helpers

Wendy talks with her grandfather.
They talk about school **helpers.**
The helpers have different jobs.

Mr. Chan drives the school bus.
He brings Scott to school.
Miss Green is the school **nurse.**
She helps when children are sick.

 # Schools Are for Everyone

This is Mrs. Gomez.
She is the school **principal.**
Mrs. Gomez says that schools are not just for children.
Schools are for everyone.

One day is Open School Day.
On another day there is a meeting.
Last week there was a book fair.
Sometimes there are ball games.
People even **vote** in this school.

10 Other Kinds of Schools

There are many kinds of schools.
There are schools for children.
There are schools for **adults**.
Some schools teach people to dance.
Others teach people to cook.

There are schools that teach
you how to fly.
There are even schools for
clowns.
You can learn many things in school.

George Washington Carver

"Start with what you have. Make something of it." A man named George Washington Carver said that. He did that too.

As a boy, Carver was not strong. He could not do hard work. So he had a small garden. He worked in it by himself. He grew many kinds of **plants**. Soon he knew a lot about them. As a man, he taught farmers. He helped them grow new plants. One was the peanut.

UNIT REVIEW

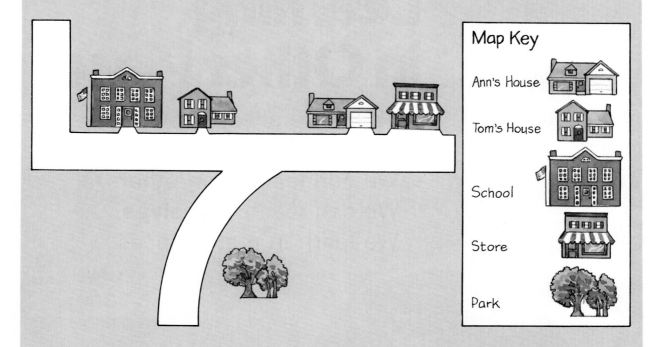

Map Key

Ann's House

Tom's House

School

Store

Park

1. Look at the map. Use the
map key.
Find Tom's house on the map.
What is next to it?
Find the park.

2. Name two school helpers.
Tell what they do.

UNIT 5

Learning in Other Places

There are always new things to learn.

We can learn from others.

We can teach **ourselves**.

We learn in many places.

Learning to Swim

People learn in school.
They also learn in other
places.
Children can learn at a lake.
These children are learning to swim.
The **lifeguard** is their teacher.

People learn to swim so they
will be safe.
Swimming is fun.
Swimming can help to make us strong.

 # You Can Learn in a Music Class

We learn about **music** at home and at school.
We learn about music in other places, too.
Music teachers give **lessons**.
They show us how to sing or play.

We must **practice** our music.
The practice may be hard.
But it is fun too.
We practice so we will get better and
better.

3 You Can Learn at a Museum

People learn in **museums**.
They can learn about long ago.

The children look at **displays**.
They read the signs.
The **guide** tells them about the display.

Museums also teach about life today.
Some museums let you touch the displays.

Museums can also teach us about the
world of the **future**.
A museum makes you think.

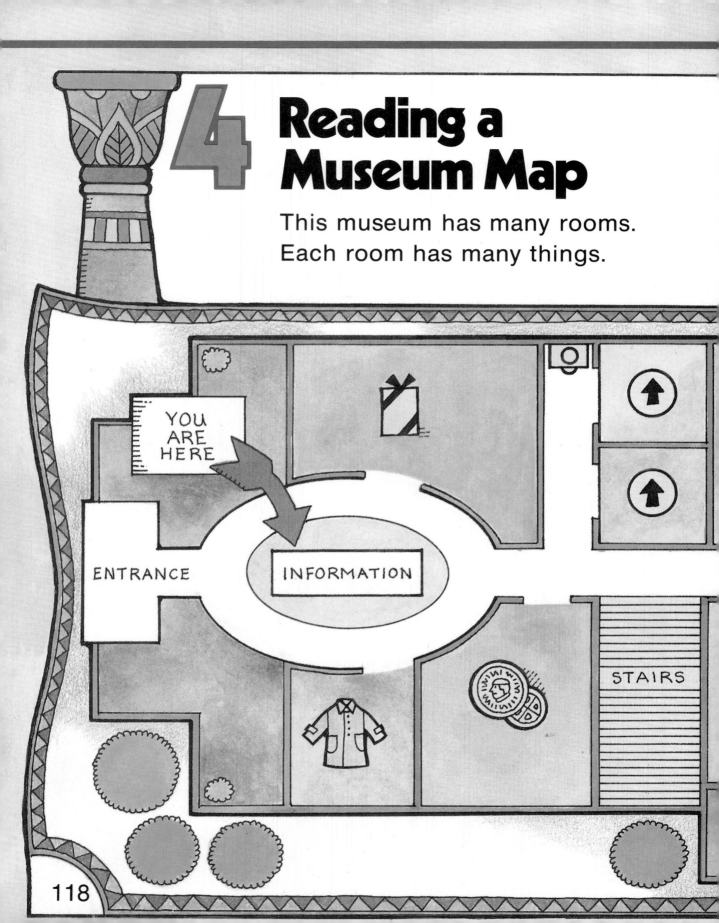

4 Reading a Museum Map

This museum has many rooms.
Each room has many things.

YOU
ARE
HERE

ENTRANCE

INFORMATION

STAIRS

The museum map shows where things are.
Use the map key to read the map.
Find the coin display.
What other displays can you find?

MAP KEY

SUITS OF ARMOR

TOOLS

ELEVATORS

COAT ROOM

REST ROOMS

DRINKING FOUNTAINS

GIFT SHOP

COINS

DINOSAURS

AUDITORIUM

5 You Can Learn Through Sports

Sports can be fun.
These children are having a **contest**.
The **coach** teaches them the rules.
He also teaches them **skills**.
The children help each other
learn.

All the children do their
best.
They show what they have
learned.
Not everyone **wins**.
But they still have fun.

6 You Can Learn on a Camping Trip

Andy's club is camping.
The children learn about nature.
They learn to do things for **themselves**.

The **ranger** guides the children.
Andy learns about plants.
He also learns about animals.
Andy takes pictures with his **camera**.

Andy shows his friends the camping pictures.
His friends learn about his trip.
They learn about nature too.

The ranger said;
"Be careful!"

"We read the directions."

"Watch out! This plant
makes you itch!"

"Keep the park clean."

"We learned songs."

Sarah Caldwell

Sarah Caldwell always loved music. But she loved acting, too. Her family took her to see plays. She liked the operas the best. The operas had both music and acting.

Sarah Caldwell wanted to lead an opera someday. She read books. She practiced leading the music. Sarah Caldwell became the leader of the Boston opera. Now Sarah Caldwell is famous. But she and the players still practice. They want their work to be even better.

1. Look at the pictures.
What is each child learning?

2. Look at these workers.
What do they teach?

Then and Now

Look at these pictures.
Tell which people lived long ago.
Tell which people live now.

128

1 Houses Long Ago

Jed lived long ago.
There were many trees where
Jed lived.
Jed's family cut some trees
into logs.
His family made a house from
the logs.

Maria also lived long ago.
There were few trees where Maria
lived.
No one made wood houses.
People used mud and straw instead.

Houses Now

Ken lives in this house.
It was made for one family.
Ken's house is made of many things.
Some things came from nearby.
Some came from far away.

Lee's house is also made from
many things.
But it is made for many families.
Lee lives in an **apartment house.**
Apartment houses can be very tall.

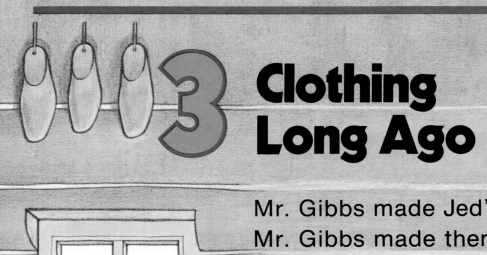

3 Clothing Long Ago

Mr. Gibbs made Jed's boots.
Mr. Gibbs made them from
animal skin.
He used tools to do this.
First Mr. Gibbs dried the skins.
Next he cut out pieces of skin.
Then he sewed the pieces together.

Maria's dress was made of cotton.
Cotton grew near Maria's house.
Her mother made **cloth** from the
cotton.
Then Maria's mother made the
cloth into **clothes.**

 # Clothing Now

Today people use machines to make clothing.

1. Machines make thread into cloth.

2. The cloth is made into clothing.

3. The clothing is sent to stores.

4. Ken's new shirt comes from a store near his home.

137

5 Communications Long Ago

Jed's family got a letter!
The letter left the city by
boat.
Then it went by **stagecoach**.
A **rider** brought the letter to town.
The **news** was old, but it was
still fun to get a letter.

Maria's people did not write.
Instead they told **stories**.
Grandfather told Maria his
stories.
Now Maria can pass on the
stories to others.

 Communications Now

Today the mail goes by jet,
train, or truck.
Bob could write his friend a letter.
It would get to his friend soon.
Bob uses the **telephone** instead.
It is fun to talk with his friend.

Sue likes to look for pictures.
She likes pictures of things that
are news.
Today the news travels fast.
How do you learn the news?

7 Travel Long Ago

Jed's family had two horses.
The horses worked in the fields.
The horses also pulled the wagon.
Jed's family used their wagon to
go to town.

Maria's family walked from place
to place.
Sometimes Maria carried things
on her head.
Name other ways things were
carried.

8 Travel Now

Ken and his family **travel** a lot.
Ken loves to ride on a **train.**
He looks out of the train window.
He sees many towns and fields.

Lee is going to visit
her uncle.
Lee is flying there
in a **plane.**
Planes are the fastest
way to travel.
They can cross our
country in a few hours.

The Earth in Space

Special planes fly into **space.**
They are called **spacecraft.**
This is how the earth looks from space.
It looks like a giant ball.

Here is another picture of the earth.
It shows the **land.**
The land is green.
The picture also shows **water.**
The water is blue.

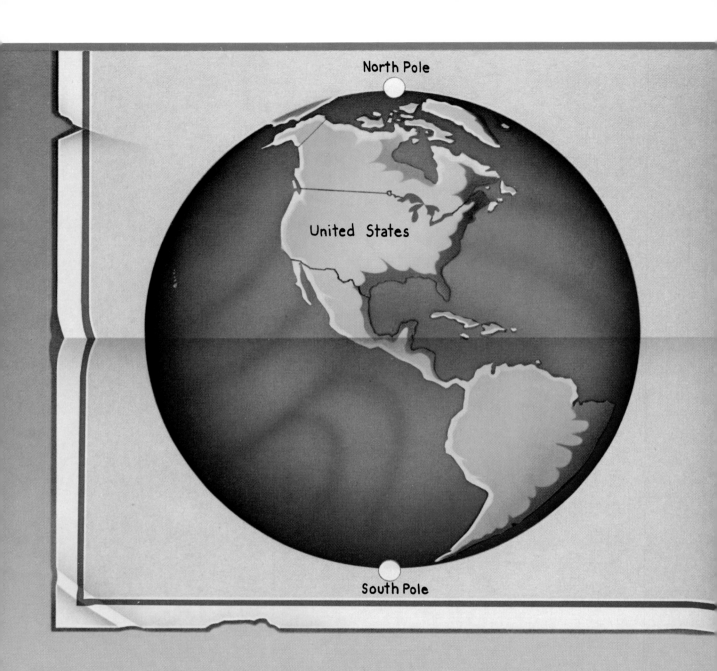

North Pole

United States

South Pole

Look at this picture.
Find the **North Pole.**
To get there, you go **north.**
Find the **South Pole.**
To get there, you go **south.**

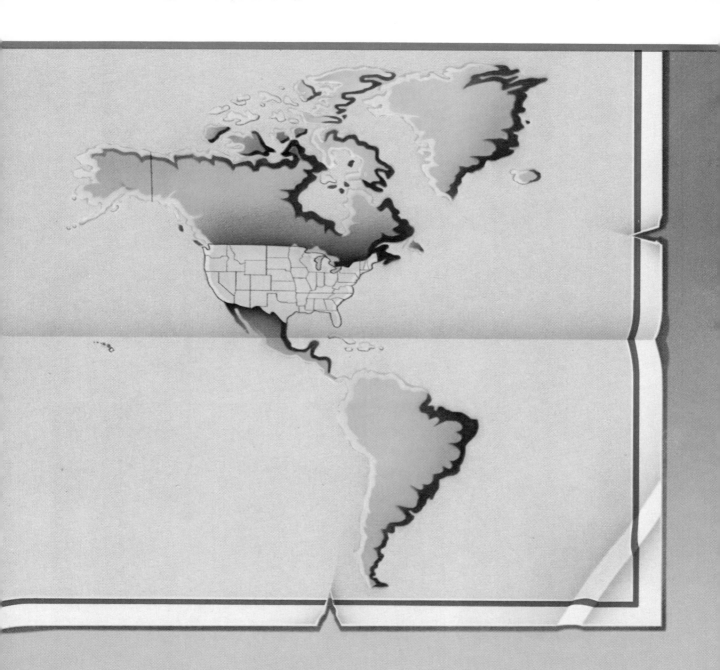

Look at this map.

It shows part of the earth.

We live in this part.

Find our country on the map.

Our country is the **United States.**

10 Space Study

Astronauts study the earth, the **moon**, and the **planets**. They study the sun and the **stars**. Astronauts work hard to learn their jobs.

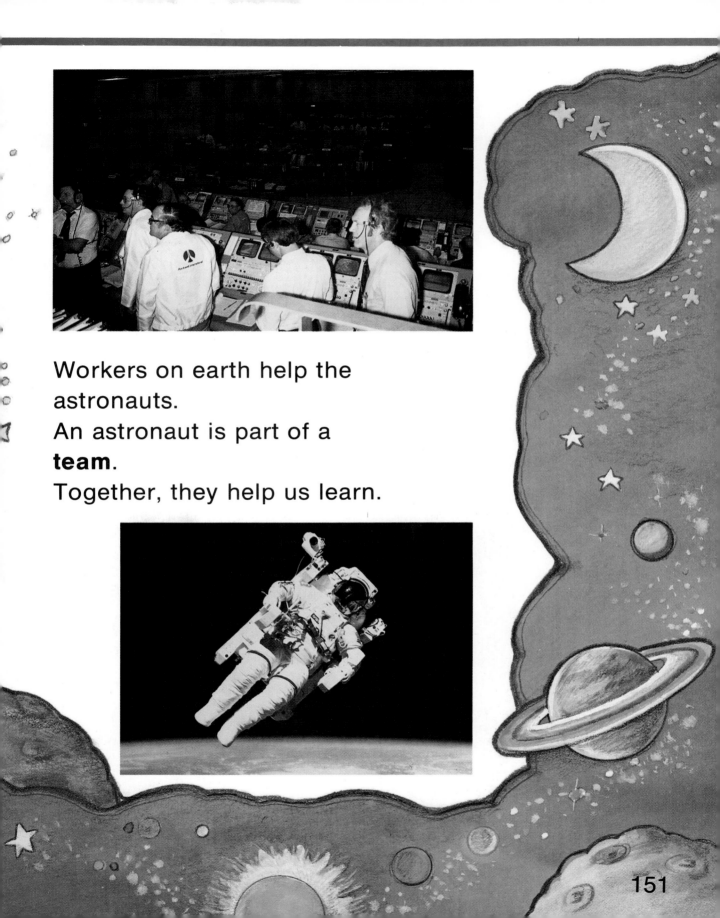

Workers on earth help the
astronauts.
An astronaut is part of a
team.
Together, they help us learn.

JOHNNY APPLESEED

The man called Johnny Appleseed lived long ago. He lived at the same time as Jed. His real name was John Chapman.

He wanted to help his country. So he planted apple tree seeds. People called him Johnny Appleseed. He planted seeds in many parts of the United States. That is one reason why so many apples grow here today.

UNIT REVIEW

1. Look at the picture.
   Which letter is on the North Pole?
   Which letter is on our country?
   Which letter is on the water?

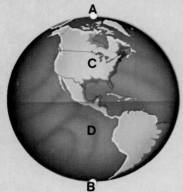

2. Which pictures show how
   people lived long ago?

PICTURE DICTIONARY

American flag

The American flag stands for the United States.

astronauts

Astronauts are people who fly in spacecrafts.

clock

A clock is used to tell the time.

clothing

Clothing is what people wear. People need clothing.

display

A display is a showing of something.

BUTTERFLY DISPLAY

earth

The earth is the planet on which we live.

food

Food is what people eat. People need food.

home

A home is a place where people live. People need homes.

map

A map is a picture of a place.

map key

A map key helps you read a map.

museum

A museum is a place where people learn about long ago and today.

nature

Nature includes all plants and animals.

North Pole

The North Pole is the place all the way north on the earth.

President

The President is the leader of the United States.

seasons

The seasons are the four parts of a year. They are spring, summer, fall, and winter.

South Pole

The South Pole is the place all the way south on the earth.

spacecraft

Spacecrafts are special planes that fly into space.

stagecoach

A stagecoach carried people and mail long ago.

sun

The sun gives light and heat to the earth.

United States

The United States is the country we live in.

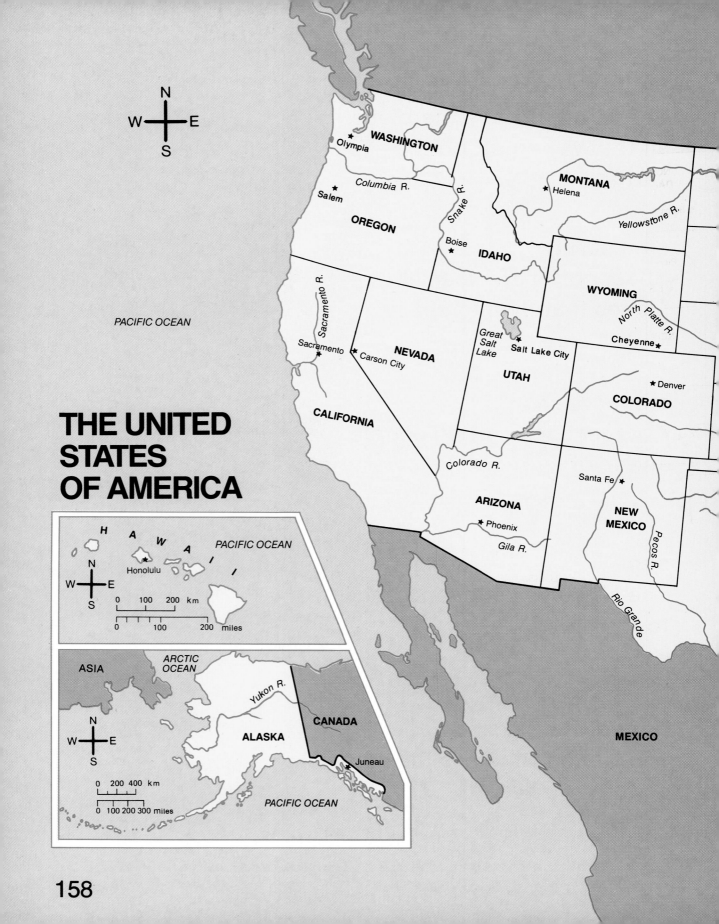

THE UNITED STATES OF AMERICA

WASHINGTON
★ Olympia

Columbia R.

★ Salem

OREGON

Snake R.

MONTANA
★ Helena

Yellowstone R.

★ Boise

IDAHO

WYOMING

North Platte R.

Sacramento R.

Great
Salt
Lake

Salt Lake City ★

Cheyenne ★

Sacramento ★

★ Carson City

NEVADA

UTAH

★ Denver

COLORADO

CALIFORNIA

Colorado R.

Santa Fe ★

ARIZONA

NEW
MEXICO

Pecos R.

★ Phoenix

Gila R.

Rio Grande

MEXICO

PACIFIC OCEAN

HAWAII

PACIFIC OCEAN

Honolulu ★

0   100   200   km

0   100   200   miles

ASIA

ARCTIC
OCEAN

Yukon R.

CANADA

ALASKA

Juneau ★

PACIFIC OCEAN

0   200   400   km

0   100 200 300 miles

CANADA

NORTH DAKOTA
• Bismarck

MINNESOTA
St. Paul ★

Lake Superior

MICHIGAN

Lake Huron

St. Lawrence R.

MAINE
Augusta ★

Montpelier ★
NEW HAMPSHIRE
VERMONT

SOUTH DAKOTA
• Pierre

WISCONSIN
Madison ★

Lake Michigan

Lansing ★

Lake Ontario

Hudson R.

Concord ★
MASSACHUSETTS
Boston ★

RHODE ISLAND
Hartford ★
Providence

NEBRASKA

IOWA
Des Moines ★

Illinois R.

Albany ★
NEW YORK

Springfield ★
ILLINOIS

INDIANA
Indianapolis ★

OHIO
Columbus ★

PENNSYLVANIA
Harrisburg ★

CONNECTICUT
Trenton ★
NEW JERSEY

• Lincoln

Ohio R.

Topeka ★

Missouri R.

Jefferson City ★

Frankfort ★

WEST VIRGINIA
Charleston ★

Richmond ★

Dover
DELAWARE

Annapolis
MARYLAND

Washington, D.C.

KANSAS

Arkansas R.

MISSOURI

KENTUCKY

VIRGINIA

OKLAHOMA
Oklahoma City •

Canadian R.

ARKANSAS
Little Rock ★

Tennessee R.

Nashville ★
TENNESSEE

Raleigh •
NORTH CAROLINA

Red R.

Mississippi R.

Columbia ★
SOUTH CAROLINA

Savannah R.

ATLANTIC OCEAN

TEXAS
★ Austin

Sabine R.

LOUISIANA
Baton Rouge •

MISSISSIPPI
Jackson •

ALABAMA
Montgomery •

Atlanta ★
GEORGIA

Tallahassee ★

FLORIDA

GULF OF MEXICO

0   100 200 300 400 500 kilometers

0   100   200   300   400   500 miles

⊛ National capital
★ State capital

159